How to Develop Good Systems for Profit?

By

Chakrapani Srinivasa

I0480530

How to Develop Good Systems for Profit?

By Chakrapani Srinivasa

Copyright 2020 Chakrapani Srinivasa

About the Author

Chakrapani Srinivasa (Padmaja), Freelance journalist from India possesses Bachelor degree in Engineering (B.E) and Post graduate in Business Management (MBA) with Distinction. He has worked as Associate Editor of 'Naradar' fortnightly journal in Chennai, India. He is the Senior Editor of the journal "The Divineness".

Contributed articles, short stories and travelogues in leading journals like Ananda Vikatan, Kumudam, Savi, Kalki, Dinamani Kadhir, Dinamani daily, Idhayam Pesukirathu and Naradar etc

He has written articles and e books through Smashwords Inc, Kindle Direct Publishing, Atlanta publications, Cooperjal publications (UK), lulu.com, ezinearticles.com, shvoong.com, iproclaim.com (USA) and TCC news (Germany).

He is the Consulting Editor: Contemporary Who's Who-Research Board of Advisers of ABI, USA.

View his books

Click to see my e books published by Amazon

http://www.amazon.com/s/ref=la_B01G3JTQ92_B01G3JTQ9
2_sr?rh=i%3Abooks&field-
author=Chakrapani+Srinivasa&sort=relevance&ie=UTF8

#Pl visit my author's page in Amazon

https://www.amazon.com/-/e/B01G3JTQ92

Preface

System is a complex of elements or components directly or indirectly related in a casual network.

Any system must have an objective or a set of objectives.

Objectives achieved through system are:

-Overall alignment of the company's business plans to the project

-Clear articulation of goals that are widely understood.

-A well established communication plan that involves the whole organization.

System is an assembly of procedures, processes united in some form of regulated interaction to form an organized whole.

"Systems are something that stay behind and can be used by anybody irrespective of who comes and who goes"

In any business operation total quality can be achieved only by standardizing each and every one of its processes – from manufacturing to advertising, from training to customer service in the form of systems.

Contents

System

System is a complex of elements or components directly or indirectly related in a casual network. Any system must have an objective or a set of objectives.

Objectives achieved through system are:

-Overall alignment of the company's business plans to the project

-Clear articulation of goals that are widely understood.

-A well established communication plan that involves the whole organization.

System is an assembly of procedures, processes united in some form of regulated interaction to form an organized whole.

"Systems are something that stay behind and can be used by anybody irrespective of who comes and who goes"-General Manager, MODI XEROX.

"Smarter management decisions are made with the help of systems"-Mr. Dutt, Managing Director, Coats India Ltd.

Above versions gives the importance of systems.

In any business operation total quality can be achieved only by standardizing each and every one of its processes – from manufacturing to advertising, from training to customer service in the form of systems.

"As liberalization unfolds, top management must set up system, which endures. In other words, systems must be institutionalized "says Mrityunjay Athreya, Athreya Management Systems.

By breaking down each activity into discrete sequential steps, the company attempts to eliminate deviations from the norm.

Quality in any business comes from maintaining these systems, irrespective of the movement of individuals in and out of the company. Every company should believe in systems, not originality.

Good performance in a business springs out by breaking down each and every function as follows:

-Manufacturing

-Advertising

-Internal communication

-Holding meetings

These should be classified as distinct systems in the organization.

Each of them is analyzed as follows:

-What is to be done?

-When it is to be done?

-How it is to be done?

Paring down the possibility of individual variations to the minimum is to be done.

Brilliance may come from innovations but consistency can be produced only by system design.

System is a complex of elements or components directly or indirectly related in a network. It has subsystems and further subsystems. We have the black box level which is some perceptible manageable level. We have the super or supra system which forms the environment in which the system operates.

"Every manager should formulate systems so that workers enjoy their job"-Pradeep Doot, Director: Videocon.

Systems should be set up to support individual initiative. Stringent guidelines and checklists should be laid down for each step of every process. Even if all people leave the organization tomorrow, operations must be continued by their replacement at the same error free levels.

Quality Systems

"The degree of success depends on the systems. If systems are not too bureaucratic, it really works"- M.D. of a MNC

Consider for example a popular Xerox Copier's method to solve a typical problem – sudden stoppages of Xerox for no apparent reason.

Following the systems laid down for treating such a complaint, the problem was sorted by the team responsible for Central Corrective Action and handed over for a solution to a cross functional team, comprising representatives from the following:

-Technical support
-Engineering shop floor
-Sales departments
-Finance department

Using the systems, each step is codified in the required manner and the problem gets solved easily and quickly.

Total quality management – super supra system

-Systems & subsystems & environment & boundary

-Senior management behavior (subsystems)

-Management practices and survey

-Four quadrant reporting

-Business goal review

-Management resource planning

-Communication

-Role, responsibility and objectives

-Confirm the role of each employee in achieving the targeted results.

-Policy deployment

-Strategic plan

-RROS

-Functional RROS

-Individual RROS

Training

-Refresher training

-Group meeting

-Leadership through quality

-Inspection

-Recognition and rewards

-Management by fact

-Statistical process control

Quality Network

-Full time resources

-Quality training

-Customer satisfaction management

-Quality improvement projects

-Competency development

Part -time Resources

-Lead by demonstrations

-Apply quality principles to daily work

-Research proficiency in business process management

Quality Policy

-Quality means providing internal and external customers with innovative products and services that fully satisfy their needs.

Standards and Measures:

-Customer satisfaction

-Measurement survey

-90 days survey

-Periodic survey

Market Share

-Market dynamics measurement survey

-Return on Assets

-Recognition and Rewards

-Quality improvement projects

-Cross functional teams

-3 tier evaluation criteria: Business results, business process, team work innovations.

-Presidents awards

-European MFG awards

Aims of a popular MNC:

To provide a complete range of document mission: processing products.   To help customers make their offices more productive.

The above system network reveals the entire sub systems, environment etc for a popular Xerox Company, which has been taken for an example.

For the above planning, the systems are devised and processed such that functioning can take place even if individuals change.

Global quality audits are used as benchmark efficacy of systems.

Manufacturing System of a leading MNC

Business Environment:

An era of opportunities opened up for a cycle manufacturing company, when a 34% antidumping import duty by the European Community priced Chinese bicycles out of the market. But while exports have zoomed, profits have been dipping steadily for this company.

The problem: Its traditional manufacturing Systems, Characterized by
-large batch production
-slow turn around

They have been unable to cope with the European markets, whose rapidly shifting consumer preferences demanded small batch production and manufacturing flexibility.

Now this company is dismantling its production systems to generate profits from quality.

"Objectives of our systems were:

-Cut lead times in order to keep pace with the customer's changing requirement better

-Boost product quality as per the customer's requirements

-Minimize costs by bringing down wastage levels and inventory." says the Managing Director of that cycle company

By tackling the above objective, "We will be covering the gamut of our operations" says it's DGM/Opn.

It would mean delivering goods on time, ensuring that they match quality standards as determined by the customer and by minimizing costs.

Sub-Systems:

Breaking down each shop floor activities into value adding and non value adding activities was done.

Restructuring manufacturing system into

- Standard bicycles
- Export bicycles
- Braced specials
- Home welded bicycles
- Rims – supplied to first 4 models

- Electroplating
- Packaging

Maintaining global quality as the limit and boundary, the manufacturing system designed by Prof. Michal Porter of Harvard Business School, worked well.

Salient points of this System

-cell/ modular layout

-dedicated plant

-seeks to avoid over production

-small batches short run rapid change over

-inventory minimization

-make to order

-low overheads

-high customer sensitivity

Best Practices for a System:

-Ask overseas customers to educate employees in quality measures

-Break up centralized manufacturing into autonomous units

-Eliminate non-value adding activities from every process

-Make every worker an internal customer of the previous one

-Set up and monitor parameters to track process quality system

- B.D. Kapur, President – Atlas

Cycle

Management System

- Managers must move from a results-only philosophy to a systems-lead-to results ethos.
- Employees must learn to use the above model, a methodology to improve processes.
- The systems must be revamped to nurture employee-participation in systems improvement activities.

Set up systems to support individual initiative, says -Walter a Shewart, Father of Management Science AT & T – Bell lab, USA.

The modern managers must be capable of managing his systems after identifying the above mentioned boundary, environment, components and objectives and have a control over the strategic planning and achieve the desired goals.

Data Flow in a Hospital

Midstate Community Hospital is a typical in and outpatient medical centre in a medium sized Midwestern town. Data entities for this hospital include patient, bed, patient room, medical procedure, physician charge and drug/item (for ex. Television rented for the patient) The Data Flow Diagram similar to that of an Accounts system for these entities in this hospital is given below:

Data Flow Diagram is a graphical representation to depict the flow of data in a CBIS. It gives a logical Data flow and not a physical data flow.

The logical Data flow in a CBIS can be explained as follows:
-Data originates from a Source and undergoes some Processing and terminates in a sink.
-The processing step may require data stored elsewhere in Data Stores, over and above what is supplied by the source.
-Similarly the output of processing may be an intermediate data store which is used for subsequent processing.

These components of a DFD can be presented graphically using the following conventions:
-A closed square box to denote source/sink

-An open rectangular box to denote intermediate store.

-A circle to denote processing

-An arrow to denote the directional flow of data

A DFD displays data flow in a Top down approach.

Therefore we start with a macro DFD and explode it into micro DFDs.

Care has to be exercised to provide clarity for each level of DFD.

Details OF DFD OF MCH:

When a patient enters for treatment in Midstate Community Hospital (MCH) he/she is FIRST diagnosed by the Physician in the Patients Room (Hospital) with the assistance of nurse and lab assistants. In the laboratory, following tests are conducted:

Lab Tests

- Blood Test
- Urine Test
- Motion Test
- Blood Pressure
- ECG

Radiography Tests

- X-Ray
- C.T.Scan

These are conducted on the patient to determine the exact health condition and to pin point the health problem.

After correct determination he/she is admitted as Inpatient under two conditions
- Critical
- Serious

If he is critical, the patient undergoes emergency treatment in Intensive Care Unit. Immediate surgery or other emergency actions are undertaken.

If the patient's condition is Serious he will be admitted in the Ward according to his
- Income
- Status (VIP, Non-VIP)
- Requirements
-

If he is a VIP, then A/C, TV then Fridge, Special Assistants will be provided.

If he is a Non-VIP and middle income group then a non-A/C room will be provided with required facilities.

If he/she is below poverty line or poor class then a room containing number of beds with common bathroom and amenities with less comfort will be provided.

If the health condition of the patient is ordinary then he requires no admission. He can be given general treatment like giving prescriptions, advices and discharged and directed to come to the Hospital after 3 days to meet the physician for confirmation of his/her recovery.

For inpatients, who are admitted will be given the required treatments as per the medical procedures – giving drips, injections, periodic tests, and after ailment/recovery they are discharged with sufficient advices and prescriptions by the physician and after clearing all medical bills, treatment charges of the Hospital.

So also critical patients get discharged after the required treatment ailments etc are given to them.

The outcome of the treatment is a cured patient.

If the treatment is successful the above flow holds good.

If the treatment fails, then the patient breathes the last and taken to mortuary and the body handed over the relatives with proper procedures like medical certificate, death certificate etc.

Methods to handle Stress

a) Is it understood that stress as overload?

b) Is certain level of stress necessary to motivate workers to perform well?

Life in the corporate fast lane can be punishing.

Stretch targets, tight deadlines and organizational politics are enough to give ulcers and insomnia to even the most unflappable.

But it's not ordinary stress, it's the one created by organizational upheavals.

The stress is powerful, omnipotent, omnipresent and inevitable. It holds the throat of the king and the masses.

- Nobody can escape from it.
- It attacks all.
- We have to secure our self with all awareness.
- Cautious people alone can override it.
- Others fall flat to it.

Stress is the consequence of loading an individual. It may be usually due to overload.

The answer is yes. But some may deny and counter argue and say it may be due to under load also. See what happens when voltage dips. Some motors burn out due to it. When voltage drops current flow increases. So also in human being under load also causes stress.

In generator when rotor runs in low voltage, high speed is seen and at times the generator windings pull out badly; so also the issues of men/women when they are overloaded.

What happens when one is overloaded?

He strains to maintain the balance of mind. He is weakening his nerves and squeezes his thought power.

Saturation occurs. Just like when a rubber band is stretched beyond its limit (over loaded) it cuts into two. The overloaded individual too breaks into pieces mentally. He is clean bowled.

It may be due to over concentration, over thinking, over muscular exertion. Totally he loses his balance.

He is over loaded.

 He is stressed!

What happens when one is under loaded?

- He feels he is neglected.
- He becomes he is unwanted.
- He may develop piles by being idle.
- He will kill his enthusiasm.
- His muscle power is wasted.

 He is ill-treated by others being idle.

"Being unwanted is the greatest disease ever experienced by Human Being"-Mother Teresa.

When Mother Teresa rose up to give her lecture after receiving the Nobel Prize, these were the words she uttered to the large gathering. Such great is the effect of being unwanted.

It is a disease. It is a dreadful disease. Incurable disease! Idleness is dangerous too.

"Idle mind is Devil!" Is it proper to allow devil to enter one's mind. No. That too in a workplace is intolerable! Violent attitude will also be kindled due to idleness.

Under load makes a man to think he is underutilized. He will under estimate his skills and talents. His potentials are wasted Human potentials are precious. When it is wasted it is a Crime!

Better utilization of man power is the vision and target of Human Resource Development. If a person is underutilized or less loaded then it reflects upon the HRD's inefficiency. Hence under load causes stress to the management and also to the individual. This is more harmful to the individual as it affects the organization as a whole.

When a man is kept under loaded then others too, who are engaged in regular work will think in an adverse manner and be reluctant to work.

This will cause stress in them and induce to remain idle like him. This will lead to bad precedence.

Under load will stress the individual, his colleagues and also the organization regarding production.

Many violent attitudes and revolutionary thinking will shoot up when an individual is idle or under loaded and cause unwanted thoughts to enter his mind and make it filthy.

This filth will cause stress.

If a man is overloaded it may cause physical harm but it will increase his experience, knowledge and vitality in that field.

His popularity will increase saying "He is a hard working gentleman".

Any amount of stress caused by overload will be lessened by this good name earned by overload.

His mind may get wild sometime due to overload but it is not so as dangerous as idleness.

Proper relaxation, Yoga and tension relieving exercises will ease out the stress. But for under load the only solution is to make him work more and engage in more relevant, reasonable manner profitable to him and to the organization.

Certain level of stress is necessary to motivate an individual.

A proud individual was telling his wife "Today I have been asked to look after Commercial department too in addition to Marketing. My boss trusts me. He trusts my capabilities. Even though there are several seniors, he has given me this special assignment!"

Look at the effect of motivation when he is overloaded.

A certain level of stress is of course caused by this new assignment.

But look at his pride.

It has built self confidence.

He is now optimistic about his potentials.

That will make him grow high and also the organization.

Stress in addition will not be considered as 'load', instead it will be 'welcomed' as gift of love, gift of trust, gift of reliability, gift for talents and admiration.

Wonderful gifts they are. He will speed up his work and exercise more efforts to fulfill his assignments. He becomes more agile.

-His wife admires.
-His subordinates get thrilled.
-His status rises to lofty heights.

He becomes a supreme man in his office and at home.

What else does a man want in his professional life than this! But adding work load or stress should be done judiciously.

- At the right time
- For the right individual

- For the right results.

Stress at certain level is necessary to make a worker perform well.

Fixing a target and cancellation of all leave near the year end to reach the targets are all stress creating activities. But it will help him monetarily. That's a benefit indirectly.

If a loose hand is held on him, then he will be doomed along with the productivity.

So, raise him and his spirit with additional load with all reasonableness and stress judiciously.

In order to help the corporate to work in coping with the changing business scenario, they have installed in their corporations user friendly software, e-mails, taxes for quick communication, cellular, pager etc which keep all in working spirit round the clock.

You cannot forget your office even in a Golf Club. The Cellular or Pager will prick you with a 'beep'. Stress is caused by these telecommunication techniques. But are these stress do any benefit to the individuals. They keep them agile and profession oriented. Even if they cause stress they are unavoidable evil doing a good work for the organization and keep the individual trim and high spirited at all times.

His status builds due to this technological equipment around him.

When status is built his motivation also rises up.

That is a good phenomenon in an organization galloping for success and prosperity.

View other books written by Chakrapani Srinivasa

HRD Instruments and Sub Systems

https://www.amazon.co.uk/dp/B00ZPHPSA0

Strange India
https://www.amazon.co.uk/dp/B07S73LCTK

Waves of Wit on the Sea of Satire: Fun Butter Jam!!
https://www.amazon.co.uk/dp/B07XF5DT72
Kohlinoor of India: Winner Virat Kohli

https://www.amazon.co.uk/dp/B07SKNRVCT

Never Forgotten Naradar Srinivasa Rao: Most Enterprising Journalist

https://www.amazon.co.uk/dp/B07NLFY73C

How to Manage Funds in an Organization?

https://www.amazon.co.uk/dp/B00Z0Q8IF8

Wonders of Nano Technology

https://www.amazon.co.uk/dp/B07D3ZP7MC

How to become a Leader?

https://www.amazon.com/dp/B08BF4HCVX

What are the Best HRD Tactics?

https://www.amazon.co.uk/dp/B07HZ7JK18

Solar Energy Plans in Tamilnadu

https://www.amazon.co.uk/dp/B01G44ZL4K

How to Forecast Manpower Needs in an Organization: You Have The Skill!

https://www.amazon.co.uk/dp/B0111GBZKK

Infrastructure in India

https://www.amazon.co.uk/dp/B0163777RW

Accountant's Role in an Organization: A book for Accountants

https://www.amazon.co.uk/dp/B00YYHDHU0

Inland Waterways and Hydro Power in India

https://www.amazon.co.uk/dp/B015NEZMXW

Strategies in an Organization

https://www.amazon.co.uk/dp/B015AV1ZWU

Conflict Management Styles and Collective Bargaining

https://www.amazon.co.uk/dp/B00Z3B9GTW

Nanotechnology Scenario in India

https://www.amazon.co.uk/dp/1520640765

Quiz and General Knowledge

https://www.amazon.co.uk/dp/B01N4M99S7

In Search of Paradise and Peace

https://www.amazon.co.uk/dp/B07C7F3XKM

Graphene -The God of Nano Technology

https://www.amazon.co.uk/dp/B07561LWTT

You Can Gain Power and Authority

https://www.amazon.co.uk/dp/B00YWY9QR8

HRD Systems and Management by Objectives

https://www.amazon.co.uk/dp/B016UC9UKC

International Conferences on Nanotechnology in India

https://www.amazon.co.uk/dp/B07BP8YLJZ

Holy Madhwa Saints: Get Divine Pleasure by Reading

https://www.amazon.co.uk/dp/B010WNBYU4

Trade Shows in India and Participants

https://www.amazon.co.uk/dp/B016PV1KS8

Collaboration and Intervention Techniques

https://www.amazon.co.uk/dp/B0110DLE8C

How to Plan Career and Quality Discipline in an Organization? Plan for Prosperity

https://www.amazon.co.uk/dp/B011GXOXIE

How to Become a Professional Manager? For You It Is Possible!

https://www.amazon.co.uk/dp/B011G4T6BM

Know About Systems and Stress in Management: Every Manager Should Know

https://www.amazon.co.uk/dp/B00YSDFE10

Process of Planning and Control

https://www.amazon.co.uk/dp/B010ZHIBJE

How to Speak Skillfully**?**
https://www.amazon.com/dp/B08BJ8PCKT

How to Supervise Efficiently?
https://www.amazon.com/dp/B08BNFYSPQ- e book

https://www.amazon.com/dp/B08BR8YYG6?ref_=pe_3052080_397514860

Click to see my e books published by amazon
http://www.amazon.com/s/ref=la_B01G3JTQ92_B01G3JTQ92_sr?rh=i%3Abooks&field-author=Chakrapani+Srinivasa&sort=relevance&ie=UTF8

www.ingramcontent.com/pod-product-compliance
Lightning Source LLC
Chambersburg PA
CBHW030547220526
45463CB00007B/3017